Endorsements for *Ghost Poetry*

These poems of honesty and intimacy are like branding irons that take possession of loss, absence, heart ache and grief. They are fire-heated with urgency and with the need to own and to proclaim what trauma does to the heart and the body. These are unflinchingly visceral poems, yet they also speak in spectral tones of how the past can haunt the present, the mind the body. Coburn speaks of both truancy and attendance and makes remarkable poetry out of the spaces between them. The poems are uncompromisingly written in their own terms. Their hard-won frankness, their grace are retrievals for hope.

Judith Beveridge

Coburn's dreamlike poems in *Ghost Poetry* conjure landscapes that are ruinous, apocalyptic and scarified. In these dark paddocks, horses and bodies bleed into one another, and the veil between external and internal worlds blurs. Coburn's raw and intimate poems are marked by a strong presence of voice: confessional, consolatory, despairing and defiant, these poems speak of impulses that are often repressed or left unsaid. Coburn deftly weighs the impulse towards harm with the yearning for recovery, reminding us, always, "what the lines have cost".

Sarah Holland-Batt

There was a point during my first reading of *Ghost Poetry* when I nearly had to stop. My breath was tight, and I felt anxious. That's how deep the emotion is within these lines. Robbie Coburn has created his greatest piece of work yet – which is saying something already, given the strengths of this phenomenal writer. This collection made me feel in exactly the way that I want art to make me feel – it brought out feelings that I needed bringing out, it hurt me in a way that also felt beautiful. It made me feel – it reminded me I was alive. I won't tell you which poem stopped me in my tracks or which lines got to me – trust me, you'll find your own. *Ghost Poetry* is an immense achievement.

Thomas Moore

Ghost Poetry

Robbie Coburn

Robbie Coburn's books include *And I Could Not Have Hurt You*, *The Other Flesh* and *Rain Season*. He has also published several chapbooks.

His poems have been published in *Poetry*, *Meanjin*, *Island*, *Westerly*, and elsewhere, and anthologised in books including *Writing to the Wire* and *To End All Wars*.

Additionally, Coburn's haiku has been published widely, including in *Modern Haiku*, *The Heron's Nest* and *Frogpond*, and anthologised in *a hole in the light: The Red Moon Anthology of English-Language Haiku 2018*.

Born in 1994, Coburn grew up on his family's farm in Woodstock, Victoria.

He is currently based in Melbourne.

Also by Robbie Coburn

And i Could Not Have Hurt You (2023)
The Other Flesh (2019)
Rain Season (2013)

Robbie Coburn

Ghost Poetry

UPSWELL

First published in Australia in 2024
by Upswell Publishing
Perth, Western Australia
upswellpublishing.com

Upswell operates in the city of Perth, on ancient country of the Whadjuk people of the Noongar nation who remain the spiritual and cultural custodians of this beautiful land. We acknowledge their continuing connection to country and express gratitude to elders past and present for their strength and creativity…Always was, always will be, Aboriginal land.

ISBN: 978-0-6455368-9-8

A catalogue record for this book is available from the National Library of Australia

Cover design by Chil3, Fremantle
Typeset in Foundry Origin by Lasertype
Printed by McPherson's Printing Group

Upswell Publishing is assisted by the State of Western Australia through its funding program for arts and culture.

For

Robert Adamson

1943–2022

Poet, mentor, friend

for n'er was dream
so like a waking
William Shakespeare, *The Winter's Tale*

I'll throw myself beneath the horses' hooves!
Arthur Rimbaud, *A Season in Hell*

Let it be known that we are all ghosts
Emma Ruth Rundle

Contents

I.

Blood Ritual

Ghost Poetry

I will be the ghost who dreams of you
until our eyes collide.
there is no map in my flesh, no doorways or windows.
no spurred heart or bruised throat when we touch.
the house where we lived is still standing.
everyone we know is there.
I bite into my tongue and say sorry
because you have already told them everything.
there is nothing you will remember
about my new bedroom
as you redress yourself
in my bones.
we sit down on the bed and speak
but you cannot hear me
and I cannot hear you.
I want to tell you what happened to me after,
what the blood and glass
was meant for. sometimes the night
makes you look like a stranger.

Blood Ritual

"I saved the pieces of you
when you fell apart."

the deepening puncture
of my fingers against paper,
writing.

I closed my eyes and it was there;

a horse I will never see again.
blackened trees fallen in a burning paddock.
knife wounds running with blood
viewed through broken glass.

beyond all distance
it was there again;

same night; pain
and the right hand rising
and gripping the left wrist
as if holding the body of a child.

I know this time it will be endless.

the inconceivable weight
of a book bound in flesh.

Hospital Theory

They do not want to die
when they leave their mother's body

as we do.
they told you every day was a word
to define what had happened
and the blood was somehow meaningful.

you were lying in the middle of the road
crying
convincing yourself the driver didn't matter
and it was all for a purpose.

and it didn't matter who found you
that way.
but you imagined it was your mother;

a mare birthing a stillborn foal
and attempting
to nurse it back to life.

Knife Diary

I woke again and heard the rain;
heavy air dissolving into two mouths,
unspeaking.

I asked myself if my body was enough
to leave behind.

blood on the branches of a pine tree
against the darkened window

where I am here alone
making a space for you.

Alcoholism

And to choose to never
leave you

and return unchanged.

the night deepening, in the instant
of colliding with the ruin of your mouth.

your skin feels like sleep
surrounding my body forever;

I want to stay with you here,
where you love my blood
as I have never known

and you are always mine.
a safety in the longing
written in your name
and suffocating my breath.

I was born in your arms.

Dream of Human Sacrifice

A dream of leaving;
the piercing scream
of a fired bullet
parting dark water.

suddenly I was a child
running a razorblade
across my arm;
frightened by the blood

and mesmerised by the trail
it left on the surface
of my skin

as if the scar was drawn
by an unknown hand
and would not follow.

not knowing I would live
inside those wounds
as if they were shelters
welcoming me,
saying

you can create a new life
and abandon your past.

no more nightmares.
no more ghosts.
no more poems.

just you here alone,
always writing the end of a story.

Oblivion

Morning has to come
at some point

you are the sole pedestrian
measuring the length of the body
trailing your shadow
under the streetlights.

it all belongs to you.
the night sky and vacant streets.
the passing cars that do not stop for you.
and the voices whispering
into the distance, especially.

and when it begins to rain
you will not seek cover
or turn back towards the room
where you are living.

you know no one can help you.
at this distance everyone is gone
and the rain is telling you something.

Dream of Scarification

Again I had drunk myself to sleep;

my mouth would not open,
the lips stitched
and incapable of protest.

a vast gathering of screaming mouths surrounded me.
I noticed my hand held a knife,
the bone and muscle exposed.

I turned away and opened my eyes –

the skin was hung before me
like a target,
stretched between two blackened trees,
the burning rain striking my veins
and entering my bloodstream.

somehow I knew the surface
of that body
was unmistakably mine.

standing before myself I lunged,
wincing as the blade drove in.
the mouths suddenly fell silent
and disappeared.

my blood moved slowly
and began to circle
around my flesh,
pooling and forming
a familiar pattern.

this time the wound
would bear your name,
my body bathed in salt.

Cutter

The last face I see
will be that of a child

learning of its own death,

a scavenger
tracing a bullet hole
in a cow's skull.

we do not know who we are.

Dream of Suicide

I want to tell you the way it will happen;

it will feel like being a child waiting
for the night to come, unafraid.

there is careful planning.

there are final words and answers
for everything.

there is a razorblade and a mirror.

somewhere else, years ago,
there is inconceivable light,
the unfamiliar bodies illuminated.

it will feel like leaving something
unnameable behind.

there is beauty in controlling the flesh,
unasked for.

there is no suffering.

there is only the figure lying
against the bathroom tiles,
tracing the slowing pulse
of an opened wrist

in a dream
where my body ends
at the moment
I recognise it as a stranger's.

Bloodletting

I wish I'd known you
before the fractured dawn
where it began

before I became an enemy
lacerating the flesh
and collecting the signs
of an ending.

the skin is like anything else
when cut;
fragile and worthless
in its temporary breathing.

I wish I'd known you
before the irreversible ruin
defined the space
left for my body
beneath the earth.

before all my life
was seen through veins.

Dream of Abortion

The night is a procedure,
unspeakable and unnamed
as you are

and will always be.
I told you in a dream
that you never lived
so that I could.

walking across an empty paddock
I saw your face in the distance,
your body made of glass.

I ran towards you,
your flesh shattering
when I pressed my hands
against your bones,

the shards lacerating the skin
of my arms,
the veins opening
and running with dark blood,
covering the paddock.

I told you I was sorry for all of this,
that I wanted to be close
to what remained of you
and die here.

I watched blood seep into glass
and realised your breath
had become a part of mine,

lying together and feeling our lives
become a widening furrow.

I will never hold your body.

I Dreamed I Saw You on a Bridge

I walked to the railing of the bridge
and looked down;
a heart receding suddenly
upon opening,
an instant of light extinguished
by distance.

the landscape without your body
lengthened;
I felt your shadow
as if it were cast
across the wires
and blanketing the concrete
around me.

you were here before the blade's edge
could sever the cables
that held my flesh
from the water's surface.

I turned away and saw myself
running blindly,
your arms forcing my body back
over the bridge's railing

before being swallowed
by the dark water.

Asylum

You still don't know
I was taken to hospital after we last spoke.
when the doctor left, satisfied I was at no risk,
I approached the bed
as if the mattress was on fire,
my hands pulling the sheet from its fixed place
and tying it around my neck.
clutching the last thing I would touch
as if it was you
remembering your finger counting
the scars on my arms.
the number higher now.
it felt I could have been anyone
as I saw my reflection
in the narrow window
after night fell.
too late for the silence to greet me,
no alarms or news for anyone.
I was already gone.
I could have died there
and it would have made no difference.
just as tomorrow, you waking
from a nightmare
and hearing that it has come true.

Burial

In the dream I am screaming.
I am holding your bones in my arms,
taking them to my family's farm
to bury them.

a crimson rain falls
and the ground is covered in ash
following a fire.

as I approach the mouth
of the property I see
the farm is no longer there;

the burnt bodies of horses
are scattered across
the blackened paddock.

there is a sudden wind
and your bones disintegrate
in my arms.

I stop screaming and close my eyes,
reaching out
as if I could hold the air.

in the dream I open my eyes
and wake up crying
because I could not save you.

Dream of Recovery

To see you finally;
I lie back in the dark and dream
of your body breathing inside mine,
the harm caused irreversible.

you've killed me slowly
as I asked you to
and everything you promised
has happened
as you said it would;

I find the room around me empty,
all the people I have known now gone.
my organs no longer serve me
as you do.

I am still unable to frame your love
as a betrayal,
knowing how many
who have loved you
die this way.

you said if it wasn't you
it would have been somebody else
waiting to kill me.
I told myself I would hold your hand
when the ending came.

the glass shatters against the table
and I run a shard across both wrists,
the veins opening and my blood
cascading down to the floor.

my body collapses, contorted
and writhing,
unable to cry out for help
and not wanting to
when you appear.

as I look up into your eyes
you lift my body and begin
to reassemble my bones.

you wipe the blood from my arms,
pressing your weight against me
and telling me to breathe,
that it is not over
and you are not leaving.

you stand me before the mirror;
I see your hands
taking hold of my face
and shaping the skin,
moulding me into a stranger.

Preparations

The upheaval in the instant
of telling you,

counting your breaths
and watching my eyes
drown your lungs.

every wound needs a place
to live inside us,
the words for leaving
a scar etched into our bodies.

I cannot find another way
of freeing you.

in the night I lie awake
as you sleep beside me –

there is safety in darkness.
you become unaware of me
as you turn over, smiling.

I see him sleeping beside you;
you wake up from a nightmare,
reaching out and taking his hand
and feeling his fingers rest
between yours.

his hands move just like mine
but he loves you as I can't.

I wish the night was unending
and I could leave no trace of myself
on your body,

the irreparable catastrophe
not waking inside my mouth.

Rape

You live in every part of me;

a waking dream of you
entering my flesh
and becoming a wound.

I wish you had told me then
that you would never leave me alone

and there was no way to drown you.

that you would lay with me
each night as I slept,

everybody we know
and how we know them
decided by you.

I wish that I had died.

my body has changed;
I feel my bones shrinking
as I dream of your breath
against my skin.

everybody in this world
who loves me
takes a part of you.

yet you are endless,
reaching for me
and taking it back,
reminding me

I do not know myself
without the violence
of your hands.

it has been years
since we have touched

but I am still a child
that will always belong to you.

Poetry

I am tired of these poems;

you can only write your own death
so many times before
you begin to plan for its arrival.

I have deepened the wound
by preserving an ending,
marking a place
for when it does come.

unable to identify
where the beginning was drawn
in my own past,

what the lines have cost.

II.
Wreck

The Saddle Maker

Fire through a column of trees, blackened trees
in a dream of horses stumbling from a cliff face.

I pulled some of the bodies back up,
the spooked herd stampeding below
without direction.
a wounded stallion, crying.
still

the ravine is no longer here
and the horses are not breathing.

there is sudden rain and an opening
in my body you could put a fist through.

as everything can be crushed by waking

a dying horse told me
that making a saddle was like painting
human skin.

Wreck

The sound of their hooves is endless
and their bodies made of blood
when you wake
one morning
and trace my spine and ribcage
in search of an opening.
your fingers gallop
across the length of my skin,
running from their own shadows.
I hear their frantic braying
as they crush my paper bones
in front of your eyes.
just as when
I was a child beneath them;
I am screaming
through mouthfuls of blood
as the wound inside me
speaks
of what you
have done.

Leaving Song

I cannot love you here.
fragments of cinder begin to fall.
it is winter and the night is coming faster.
I could not see the air escaping, saying
there is life beyond this room,
the notion of longing for this space
when it becomes irretrievable
and the emptiness of arriving there.

I have thought about leaving, again
the knife to my throat in the drive of the day's arrival,
feet crossing the street towards everywhere and nowhere.
I have not told you
before, your eyes collapsing and never returning,
the way I love your body
when I am no longer holding it there

and of the earth opening around you
where you are not sleeping
when you are not here.

Brand

Most of the time the paddock opens around you when you reach its centre,
the grasses and concealed pathways at your feet barely contained by the wires
the dying trees and eroded dams, and the veins of the city still years away.
interminable silence from every side before great cracks appear in the clouds
above your head, widening as a dark rain enters the morning
then the slow run of startled cows gathered on the hillside in the distance
on the next property you must never cross.

back at the farmland's mouth, progressing down the driveway
as you follow the noise, watching the horses being ushered
into the stockyards beneath the teeming rain
and led into the corral where he holds the smoking, steel poker;
that blackened doorway suddenly closing with the sound
of flame bitten by the water's surface.

you will remember and hear it again, years later,
the way the horse had fallen and cried out, its mouth almost human.

Horse Womb

Saliva joining the hay on the stall's floor
and becoming a new earth;
the mare collapsed exhausted
in the back paddock
after months of carrying that weight.

no movement then but her pulsating flanks,
the bucket of water she drinks from
when I hold it before her,
the snorting and trembling body I speak to
that never hears me.

no light for hours, the night a vacuum
where the shed is the earth's distance
beneath the bulbs flickering
under the tin roof.

slowly, him reaching between the mare's thighs
and his face changing.
An ageing child, I cry for hours
after I watch his shaking hands

pull the lifeless filly
from the dark mouth.

Pasture

Words are not chosen
in the breaking of our emberless dawn,
the weatherboard house collapsing
beneath winter's drive of dark rain.

no one here
as depression's shade again encroaches
in the dying light –

the stilled air beyond this room,
where wild brumbies begin to move
silently between us
progressing into the distance

as outside, two years ago,
an unbridled stallion we cannot name
runs until it is lifeless.

Geography of a Horse

One morning you notice the heaving curve of their flanks
as they halt suddenly, exhausted
before the oversized ribcage is revealed
and you count the protruding bones
with your tiny hand.

They Lie About Your Death

They never call your death a suicide.

you were unwell in the weeks
before the accident
of your leaving

and your judgement
had faltered;

each day you would wake
and grind the grasses
into the dirt
of the paddocks,
speaking to the horses
while you searched the landscape.

you found a place
to conceal your bones
in the back pasture
where you had ridden
your pony as a child.

in a dream you told me
men don't use guns and knives
on their bodies,
wouldn't tell me how many times
you took the rifle from its case
in the shed
and pressed the barrel
against your chin.

they lie about this too.

I know the urgency
of your planning,

when winter encased the property
in frost,
crows circling the disturbed surface
of the farmland –

that cold June morning
when you drove your tractor
into the dam
and let it pin you
under the water.

Carousel Horses

Hooves scraping the hard floor,
their manes and tails flaying
the carousel's rotating centre
as it moves in a constant circle.

I hear their frantic screams
as they attempt to run,
a pole piercing each of their spines
and fixing them to the ground
and sky.

I reach out for them as they pass,
one horse after another
crying and throwing their bodies
from side to side,
torn flesh weeping
around the furrow
and stripping skin
from their backs.

I take hold of one of the poles
and run beside the carousel.
the poles too are made
from their flesh,
fixed and unmoving.

I cry out to them and say
I want to take their place
if it means to save them,
tear the poles from the wounds
and set them free.

I can hear them speak together here
in response,
each word an anguished shriek;

they tell me the carousel
will never stop spinning,
and they have always been here
moving in this torturous circle.

they say the carousel is one body
powered by their blood

and that they must continue
to buck in mid-air forever,
dreaming of the moment
their bodies cease to move.

Rodeo Haiku

Midday shower
the rider unconscious
under the bull's hooves.

A Dead Horse

There is a paddock I love in particular
where the grass no longer grows,
too long trodden under the weight of horses
and resigned only to dirt and depressions in the earth.
and the foal my father reared, who died in infancy
buried somewhere there, each eroded furrow
like the scar of a tongue crying to be heard
as words betrayed me and rendered me lost once more.
wind revolves like a mare's breath across the pasture
in the land I know which you refused to walk;
the burnt earth lined by hoofprints
as I walk further from myself to find you.
and being unable to touch you now,
all we ever knew of one another
like that foal's corpse concealed in the earth.

Mine

And the dawn still comes without you.

the day's airless dark that surrounds me
from every side
where the paddocks become
an endless voyage into nowhere.

I walk on, again, the only voice my own
murmuring for my knees to break
at the earth's mouth.

I am afraid.

I drive alone across the freeway,
beyond the cars and the thousands of lives
carried towards nowhere

I am here
and you could be anywhere.

Foals

The truck's tyres persisting
down a country road
and entering the property.

we make it home
the winter rain unchanging,
and morning turning

from the float
towards the horse yards.
I loved to study the hoofprints

washed away and refashioned by yours
as you walked ahead,
the silence dissipating slowly

as I followed you
your gumboots making a space
for our feet in the wet grass

like two newborn foals
teaching one another
how to walk.

Hell

The murmur of gums.

trampled earth, roots of grasses
never ascending
embedded in featureless
paddocks

the crude carvings
in the trees
(even these
will forget you)

unchanged fence posts
tangled, misshapen
wire stilled
as you near

the decayed veranda
leading you to
the wooden door
lying ajar –
the silence of the unmoving
night air,
the blackened glass
of open windows.

the absence.

Rodeo

And now the day clearer
in the unthinkable, nameless air
where I may have died in the night
and you are not alerted and not questioning.

I remember you here as you are there,
the way your heart murmurs as if it were unbalanced
and not a part of you
that midnight's calamity to the arrival of hands
carrying you towards your flesh
and mine.

one night you dreamed you were older
and saw the house burning around you
the walls shrinking as you began tearing them away –
the night was too dark for you
and I was never born
in that hell eclipsing your birth.

remember we would wish time was not illusory
and not drenched in all the lives we had lived before
the unforgiving landscape where time buried us
in the whitening night air.

what did you call me and what did she feed you
that I could not counter
that parasitic voice you willed into our lives
which burns my skin at this distance.

within you and from where I am
in the dawn burning away beyond your gaze
where I have died and been forgotten in an instant.

I see it all, believe me.
from where I am lying
I have never loved you.

I can see my sleeping body vanishing
where all the eyes have hungered for
becomes as it always was.
even you
I see even the emergence of catastrophe
ultimately means nothing

even the connected bodies mean nothing.

Stock

Again dark.
the numbered fencelines
restricting the horses,
rusted barbed wire pricking
the fingertips

for hours the shadows lifting
to reveal the night sky
strung out across the grasses
a sudden braying entering
in deliberate pulses
the heat of their breath
indistinguishable
when the wires begin to stir
as they run from us –

I am nothing
more than a presence
with hands and a voice
to bring them closer;
the impenetrable silence
when the paddock wakes.

After the Grassfire

The rain eases, sleeping dogs, consistent wires
falling on the burnt-out farmlands
everywhere the charcoal grasses compressed

the horses, at a distance from the stables
cowering beside the trailer
the night hung limply across the hours. again

I thought of you gone in the greying landscape,
that stillness afterwards as the animals fled
into the smoking hills. the horizontal trees covering
the blackened earth. I still

cannot identify your absence as grief
against the darkening sky, overgrown, burnt weeds
consuming all space where the light
cannot filter through, turning

to hear your name spoken in my tongue,
the sound of an animal's scream
in the wind.

The Wheat Search

That unbearable light glaring down onto the silo's roof
as I climbed the thin ladder to check for old wheat;
finding nothing in that dark circle
I slid into the depth of the silo's mouth
to hide from my parents and the surrounding paddocks,
their skin of silence speaking no words of my childhood.
stuck, I wondered when the farm, like every one of us,
would be gone.

A Farm Dream

Instead of moving, I tell myself that the farm knows me,
the soft wind coming off the dark mountains searching for my face
and finding a break in my body specifically.
I have only what life here can prepare, drunk and in sleep,
a storm gathering by the time I wake alone inside the cold,
    weatherboard house
as we undress and make love for the final time, years ago,
in a flat we shared in the city;
consistent rain now as all desire dies in the dark,
the vibration of barbed wire as the horses begin to shiver outside.

Horsesong

Every afternoon it happens –

I see a horse standing in a paddock
in the rain
outside my window
not knowing why it is standing there

the bones of animals buried
beneath its hooves.

one day soon it will happen.

it will rain endlessly
and I will not be here.

III.

Straw Horses

Love Song

And the empty streets filling with rain;
a presenceless form passing
beneath nameless buildings.

everything has a place
set for us.

unknown to you and known
before I can speak your name.
in the unbearable dawn
where I cannot touch you.

how often I have lived here alone.
somewhere

a transfiguring voice telling me
the names for our lives
and the meanings for the names.

it feels like you could be born again
and remember waking
for the first time.

I cradled your body in a dream.

Torture

I want to hold you until
your body becomes my own.

I want to touch your tortured bones
as if my hands were gauze.

in the night the walls are silent
and become a wound.

the mirror returns and shows me
the blood you cannot see,

a scarred figure stolen
from your hands.

again you are hidden.
again you ache.

the silence appears and pain
encases your skin like glass.

Dream of Rain

I remember the dream
of you telling me
you were afraid of the rain
and what it meant;

no movement or light for hours
in this world with no place for us;
everything uncertain
in my frail voice following you back
into a darkness my hands
could not touch.

my body feels smaller in the night;
when I can forget the coming dawn
around your sleeping skin.
I can see your face in everything
and write your name in my own past.

I told you the rain, like love,
was reaching us both at this distance.
that it was the same rain.
that it meant our bodies could wake
and start again.

you were not speaking
but I could hear you answer.

Songbird

I searched the names
and photographs
until it came into focus;

the room was empty
but I knocked anyway

knowing you had slept
there.

I'd be there still if
I could have chosen;

a dream of your mouth
and body opening

and singing, endlessly,
one winter night

when you return to that door
and find me.

Apology

The night sky is empty
when I wake, unnoticed,
and make my way through
the lifeless house.
I am the sole face you can see
behind the dirty window,
the one still blurry with rain.
you forget you will die
when you are in love.
I'm sorry if it's too much.

Pure

Writing a poem
feels like
writing
your name.

Love Poem to a Razorblade

As a child I knew
I could keep you hidden.

I turned away from the past
and saw your mouth open
and cover me.

you told me love wasn't a word
to be spoken
but a scar cut into the surface
of the body.

anybody you love in this world
will mark you.

I believed you;
each promise immovable,
every moment between us
carved into permanence.

even when you were taken
you have never left me –

the blood was ours,
every night we were alone,
silently holding you in secret.

Horse of God

I am waiting again while the night comes
circling and directionless.

my breath riderless, carrying the knife-wielding hand
closer towards the wrist
and faltering before the stilled mouth of dark blood
untouched by the trees, unmolested by the violent grasses

I would like to be like the sun, faceless and distant again,
burning unbridled inside the sky's ceiling and braying silently
a long night in a city bar traced across the paddock's edge
and forever returning to try again.

night comes, night comes fast
drowning the rider first and then the nag
you say your brother has killed himself
and I am the murderer
I am a drunk and a drug addict.
without a rider the horse spooks
as gunfire sounds inside your skull and claims you
drowned words fading with the hooves
pounding against a stark dawn.

a horse without dreams of childhood trembling
in the cold air until being taken
and forced into a barren field
a horse running wildly into nothingness.

I thought my eyes opening and closing
in the humid night were a passage to forgiveness.
I thought I was somebody else.

Hole in the Earth

This is the air reflected on hell's ceiling
in the field where they buried you:
the dirt without foundation, prying open a space.
how soon the wind dies down when alone,
how the night moves faster
watching the sky become the past.
hours without sound;
you become the rain
the cold air that gathers before sleep
and, somehow in the darkness, makes you real.
and still unable to see you here;
the anguish of knowing you are there.

Dark Nativity

The sound of retching first,
then of crying.

I followed your voice and found you
lying on the floor, trembling.

holding you, I stared
into the toilet bowl
at the discharged lining
of your womb;

the foetal membranes
and clots of blood
shaped like a child.

Collapses of Breath

Riddled with distance cannot remember the momentary framing of time
without this connection the day palls itself against thoughts consistent drive
as the imagination preys on the senses unceasing recollection
again emerges restrictions pulse along the nerve ends
whatever passion has exhausted cannot be revived
skin worn by a harsh distance in the breath dancing across your face
where you rest alone in your body I hear your voice before you answer
I interpret the silence traced along your breath with your flesh in its course
of abandon when winter comes your skin withstands the wind's visitations

it has been months since I have touched you all longing sitting down
inside the body your expressions recurring
I cannot remove your body cannot take your hands from my skin
your promise of permanence I predicted would collapse in the drive
of your ambition for an emptiness you felt belonged to you
you could not find a love of yourself my love of you fracturing within your irises
still I love you never forgetting the rise and fall of your chest beside my body

these days assault the skin with exposure to regret knowing completely
severing all ties to your body and remaining unchanged
I cannot silence this urgency beyond the contortion of time

my body fails at this vast distance the blood ceases
does not pulse running along the veins with the unending uncertainty
of waking the distant positioning of my body with no way back to you.

Absence

The room was unchanged,
the night windless.
I wanted to love the aloneness
of my body without you
and the absence of your voice,
your face obscured by
the unmoving trees against
the window.
I could almost perceive
an immeasurable distance,
knowing that I would wake
expecting to find you,
my body
preparing to leave.

Desire

Windowless rooms.
black house
welcoming
my body. one day

the nights forget us.

the running blood.

the pulse in your wrist
as I take your hand.

your footsteps
as you enter a room.

every day the light
dimmed
beneath the weight

of these hours

as I imagine
your skin.

Dream of Longing

You live inside the silences so easily.

my body trembles each time
I reach for you,
a horse picking at a fence
attempting to break through
and failing.

I heard a voice telling me
there was a reason for all of this,
and the ruin was temporary;

the smell of alcohol,
the imprint of a human skull
in fractured glass.

the silence between us
unbroken.

Dark Time

An illusion of feathers
falling in the night.

from the ethanol's betrayal,
each word I have spoken
a mistake.

you said I am not worthless
and my mind is the murderer,

yet you still do not care
that I am here.
I see a sheet placed over my eyes
that you cannot touch
or ever know existed.

I wish that I could have chosen
another body.

I am still the ghost you have forgotten,
walking, numb and waiting for you
in a dream

where you wake me
from my death

and make a bed for me
in your hands.

Poem to a Body

I dreamed
I could hold your ribcage
until the distance
was suspended,
all pain in your breath
passing through me
and ending.

Straw Horses

And again the rigid dawn
again the morning
at the point of waking
where the impenetrable hours revolve
and rebuild you
dressed in old skin
these bodies are strangers
disappearing into separate fields
like straw horses in a thunderstorm.
the paddock will end
no matter how slowly we walk.
no matter how my mouth is wounded
each time I kiss you.
no matter the ache of our soaking bodies
and heaving throats
when I say love will drown you
to the shivering bones,
to the town within your flesh I enter
to the backyards where water pools
in the broken earth's basin.
I can call you and use your name
as refuge
your arms as a farmhouse
becoming a bonfire
at the edge of knowing
where I could invent you again
and relearn the violence
of your mouth
like the pounding
of horses' hooves trampling us
because they do not know

we are lying there
in the paddock;
take my spine as a rein
make my blood a trail
for you to ride.
look back and forget
the pulse of the fencelines closing in,
our skin burning
when we touch the dark rain.
when I watch desire drive
your scarred body free.
when you can
forgive the unchanging dawn.
forgive the burning rain.
forgive the horses colliding
with your childlike flesh
puncturing
your drowning lungs.
forgive me.

Last Poem

I walked outside towards
my deathbed,
making a path to the bridge.

you were waiting there;

as if your hands
were holding my shoulders
and lifting me above the water,
readying yourself
to release my body.

the accident of my life
reflected in your shadow,
covering me as I begin to fall.

you tell me it is too late
to walk home and try again.

Acknowledgements

Some of these poems were previously published in *Coffin Bell*, *Expat*, *Four Hundred and Two Snails: The Haiku Society of America Members' Anthology 2018 (edited by Nicholas M. Sola)*, *Holy People*, *Meanjin*, *Quadrant*, *Rochford Street Review* and *Uneven Floor*. Thank you to the editors.

Gratitude and love to Robert Adamson, Jeanne Ryckmans, Michele Seminara, Terri-ann White, Carly-Jay Metcalfe, Shelby Morgan, Timothy Lee, Emily Butcher, Claire Miranda Roberts, Thomas Moore, Michael Salerno, Dimitra Harvey, Sarah Holland-Batt, Judith Beveridge, Lou Verga, Joe Rullo, Luke Best, Jo Langdon, Emerald Cornwall-Jones, Charlotte Grant, Elly-May Barnes, David Rankine, Josh Grech, Leanne Neill, Madelaine Abela, and Kaylen Court.

Thank you and love also to Sharon, John, Matt and David Coburn, and Claire Allen.

About Upswell

Upswell Publishing was established in 2021 by Terri-ann White as a not-for-profit press. A perceived gap in the market for distinctive literary works in fiction, poetry and narrative non-fiction was the motivation. In her years as a bookseller, writer and then publisher, Terri-ann has maintained a watch on literary books and the way they insinuate themselves into a cultural space and are then located within our literary and cultural inheritance. She is interested in making books to last: books with the potential to still be noticed, and noted, after decades and thus be ripe to influence new literary histories.

About this typeface

Book designer Becky Chilcott chose Foundry Origin not only as a strong, carefully considered, and dependable typeface, but also to honour her late friend and mentor, type designer Freda Sack, who oversaw the project. Designed by Freda's long-standing colleague, Stuart de Rozario, much like Upswell Publishing, Foundry Origin was created out of the desire to say something new.